TOUGH DOGS

ROTTWEILERS

Julie Fiedler

The Rosen Publishing Group's
PowerKids Press™
New York

For Sal and Pop

Published in 2006 by The Rosen Publishing Group, Inc.
29 East 21st Street, New York, NY 10010

First Edition

Editor: Jennifer Way
Book Design: Elana Davidian

Photo Credits: Cover © Lynn M. Stone/naturepl.com; p. 4 © Gerard Lacz/Animals Animals; p. 7 © Colin Seddon/naturepl.com; p. 7 (inset) © Jim Craigmyle/Corbis; p. 8 Cameraphoto Arte, Venice/Art Resource, NY; p. 11 © Time Life Pictures/Getty Images; p. 12 © Alexandra Day/Corbis; p. 15 © Ronnie Kaufman/Corbis; p. 15 (inset) © Ralph A. Clevenger/Corbis; p. 16 © Image Source Limited/Index Stock Imagery, Inc; p. 19 © Gail Shumway/Getty Images Inc; p. 20 © David Turnley/Corbis.

Library of Congress Cataloging-in-Publication Data

Fiedler, Julie.
  Rottweilers / Julie Fiedler.— 1st ed.
     p. cm. — (Tough dogs)
  Includes index.
  ISBN 1-4042-3118-8 (lib. bdg.)
 1. Rottweiler dog—Juvenile literature. I. Title.

 SF429.R7F54 2006
 636.73—dc22

                                        2004025434

Manufactured in the United States of America

Contents

Rottweilers are popular working dogs in fields such as guarding or police work. They are also popular household pets. Although some people are afraid of Rottweilers, the breed is not naturally mean.

Meet the Rottweiler

The Rottweiler, often called the Rottie, is a bold **breed** of dog known for its bravery and strength. Rottweilers are also known for their intelligence, readiness to work, and **obedience**. Because the breed can be easily trained, they are often entered in many different kinds of contests. These events include herding, obedience, and cart pulling. These are all activities that show their many talents.

Rottweilers can seem scary, but do not let their big size fool you. Rottweilers are very faithful, making them great companions and pets. They are very protective of their owners, which is why they make such great guard dogs. Their sweet nature and their high energy make them a valuable breed for many different activities. This book will teach you about Rottweilers and how to take care of them.

What a Rottweiler Looks Like

The easiest way to recognize Rottweilers is by their markings. They have black coats with short, stiff hair and rust-colored spots on the **muzzle**, throat, chest, legs, feet, under the tail, and in a small spot above each eye.

Rottweilers are large, sturdy dogs with powerful bodies. They are very strong and can weigh 80 to 125 pounds (36–57 kg). These powerful dogs have big heads and broad chests. Male dogs are usually bigger than females, but generally Rottweilers measure 22 to 27 inches (56–69 cm) tall. When they are puppies, most owners choose to have the dogs' tails docked, or cut, to be short and stumpy. This was done in the past to many working breeds to lessen the chances of the dog's tail getting hurt while doing activities such as running through the woods.

A Rottweiler has a black coat with rust-colored markings. Inset: This Rottweiler puppy has markings like an adult's. The puppy will one day grow into a sturdy, well-built adult.

The mastiff, shown in this painting, is a breed of large dog that was common during Roman times. The mastiff is the ancestor to many breeds of large dogs, including Rottweilers.

Ancestors of the Rottweiler

The Rottweiler's **ancestors** were herding dogs. More than 2,000 years ago, the Romans had a large breed of dog called a mastiff. These dogs were very strong and were often used for herding, as guard dogs, and in battle. Around A.D. 74, the Romans occupied other parts of Europe, such as Germany and Britain. As the Romans marched through different lands, they needed a supply of food, so they took livestock with them. The large herding dogs helped the Romans drive cattle. These dogs also kept watch over the cattle and helped keep them from harm.

When the Roman Empire ended hundreds of years later, the Romans returned to Italy and left many of these herding and guard dogs behind. These dogs were **bred** with sheepdogs over the next thousand years and are believed to be ancestors of today's Rottweilers.

History of the Rottweiler

The Rottweiler gets its name from a town in Germany called Rottweil. In the 1800s, this town was a center for trade, especially livestock. Because Rottweilers were such great herding dogs, the butchers who lived there used the breed to drive cattle to and from the marketplace. On the road back from the marketplace, the butchers used the Rottweilers to help them guard their money from thieves. These popular dogs were known as the butcher's dog.

Later that century Rottweilers became less popular, and the breed almost died out. By the end of the century, the breed's popularity rose again in Germany as Rottweilers became valued for their intelligence and strength, as well as their ability to work as police dogs. Rottweilers were **introduced** in the United States in the 1920s. In 1931, the first Rottweiler was listed with the American Kennel Club.

Rottweilers have won many dog show competitions. The Rottweiler in this picture won the Best of Breed at the Westminster Kennel Club show in 1964. He appeared in Time magazine.

Alexandra Day wrote a number of children's books about a Rottweiler named Carl. In this picture from the 1996 book Carl's Baby Journal, Carl is measuring a child. Many Rottweilers have a gentle nature, which makes them a good choice of pet to bring into contact with children.

The Rottweiler Today

Today Rottweilers have many different uses. They are considered one of the best breeds to work as a guard dog. Rottweilers also help with different kinds of police work, such as guarding and tracking. They have a sharp sense of smell, which makes them very valuable on search and rescue teams, which help find people who are lost. They are also good at helping police find illegal items, such as drugs.

Though the Rottweiler is often considered a tough dog, the breed can be very gentle. Rottweilers are used as guide dogs for blind people. Because of Rottweilers' gentle natures, many people also use them for **pet therapy** work in hospitals and nursing homes to lift patients' spirits. The breed also does well in contests that measure their abilities, such as tracking, herding, and obedience.

A Tough Breed?

Rottweilers are large, powerful dogs. Some people are afraid of them because they think of Rottweilers as **aggressive** guard dogs. It is true that Rottweilers make good guard dogs. That is because they are faithful to and protective of their owners and are easily trained to do tasks, such as guarding, for their owners. They are not mean dogs by nature. Some Rottweilers may act unfriendly around strangers, but it is important to know that this powerful breed is also loving and gentle. This breed is good with children, and they make wonderful family pets. They even carry out many public services in police work and patient care.

Some careless owners mistreat their Rottweilers or teach them to be aggressive. Owners must be responsible and provide their Rottweilers with proper care and training.

With proper training and lots of love, Rottweilers can make gentle household pets. Inset: Dogs who have been trained by careless owners or mistreated may become aggressive.

15

Rottweilers have lots of energy and like to run. They can be good pets for people who are very active and like to have company while they exercise.

No matter what breed of dog you have, it is important to care for it properly. Good care requires providing housing, water, healthy food, and lots of love. Rottweilers have short, stiff coats, and their owners must **groom** them regularly. This helps the Rottweilers' fur stay smooth and clean. Owners must also make sure to take their dogs to visit the **veterinarian** for regular checkups.

Rottweilers have lots of energy and must get plenty of exercise each day. If Rottweilers do not get enough exercise, they may develop bad habits such as digging or chewing. Part of the proper care of Rottweilers also includes proper training.

DOG SAFETY TIPS

- Never approach a dog you do not know.
- When introducing yourself to a dog, offer the back of your hand for the dog to smell.
- Speak softly, not loudly. Move gently, not suddenly.
- Never try to pet a dog through a fence.
- Never bother a dog while it is sleeping, eating, or sick.
- Do not pull at a dog's fur, ears, or tail. Never tease or hit a dog.
- Never approach a dog that is growling or showing its teeth. Back away slowly. Yelling and running can cause the dog to chase you or to act aggressively.

Training a Rottweiler

Rottweilers must begin to be trained when they are about six months old. Once Rottweilers become adults, it can be hard to handle and train them because of their size and strength. There are five commands every dog should learn. These are *sit*, *stay*, *heel*, *down*, and *come*. Learning these commands, as well as additional training, provides Rottweilers with a chance to use their intelligence and energy.

Another important part of raising a healthy Rottweiler is **socialization**. Socialization involves introducing Rottweiler puppies to different settings, people, places, and dogs with careful **supervision**. It is important to introduce them to many sights, sounds, and smells, so they will not act aggressively out of fear. Most Rottweilers are good around new people if they are properly socialized when they are young.

18

Socialization is an important part of raising a dog. This can keep the dog from acting aggressively out of fear and helps dogs be good around people and other dogs. The Rottweiler on the left is playing with a Weimaraner. Each dog is acting toward the other in a friendly way, a result of proper socialization.

Rottweilers have worked in search and rescue and become heroes.
The Rottweiler here is helping rescue workers look for people in rubble from
a fallen building.

Brave Rottweilers

Rottweilers have carried out many brave deeds. One brave Rottweiler is Samantha, a family pet. Several years ago Samantha went on a walk with Blake, a three-year-old boy, who wandered into the woods and got lost. Samantha helped him **survive** a cold night by laying on top of him to keep him warm. The next day Samantha led Blake to safety. Because of her intelligence and bravery, Samantha was made an honorary member of the local rescue crew.

A Rottweiler named Jake saved his owner from drowning. Jake and Jeffrey were playing outside when Jeffrey fell into a pond. When his mother came outside, she saw that Jake had saved Jeffrey from drowning. Rottweilers like Samantha and Jake have saved many lives and are true heroes.

Many famous people have owned Rottweilers, including actor Will Smith, singer Stevie Wonder, and actor Shannen Doherty.

What a Dog!

In 2004, more than 17,000 Rottweilers were listed with the American Kennel Club. Many of these Rottweilers are working dogs. Rottweilers are very popular and are ranked as one of the top 15 breeds in the United States.

Rottweilers are a wonderful breed of dog that carries out many public services. From their work with police to their work as therapy dogs, Rottweilers have shown themselves to be caring and loving. Rottweilers have also been winners in many contests, such as obedience or herding. It is important to respect this noble, brave, and intelligent breed.

One night a Rottweiler named Carlee was found in a parking lot. She did not have any tags. A woman pulled over and took her home. She was not able to find Carlee's owners, so she decided to adopt Carlee. She noticed that Carlee had a sweet nature and trained her for therapy work. Carlee's gentle nature made her suited to the task of lifting the spirits of patients at a local hospital.

Glossary

aggressive (uh-GREH-siv) Ready to fight.

ancestors (AN-ses-terz) Kin who lived long ago.

bred (BRED) To have brought a male and a female animal together so they will have babies.

breed (BREED) A group of animals that look alike and have the same relatives.

groom (GROOM) To clean someone's body and make it neat.

introduced (in-truh-DOOSD) Brought into use, knowledge, or notice.

muzzle (MUH-zuhl) The part of an animal's head that comes forward and includes the nose.

obedience (oh-BEE-dee-ents) Readiness to do what you are told to do.

pet therapy (PEHT THEHR-uh-pee) When people use animals to help them deal with certain problems.

socialization (soh-shuh-luh-ZAY-shun) Learning to be friendly.

supervision (soo-per-VIH-zhun) Watching over carefully.

survive (sur-VYV) To stay alive.

veterinarian (veh-tuh-ruh-NER-ee-un) A doctor who treats animals.

Index

Web Sites

Due to the changing nature of Internet links, PowerKids Press has developed an online list of Web sites related to the subject of this book. This site is updated regularly. Please use this link to access the list:
www.powerkidslinks.com/tdog/rottweil/